About this book

Kelly Goes Back to School: More Science on Coronavirus is written to help families navigate the transition back to school as safely as possible during a pandemic. Key concepts including antibody testing, phased reopening, contact tracing, and hybrid school models are discussed through Kelly's eyes as a curious eight-year-old. As each of Kelly's questions are answered with accessible explanation and beautiful illustration, families and children will learn and discuss how to approach the coming months bolstered by evidence, reassurance, and information.

Kelly Goes Back to School: More Science on Coronavirus

Copyright © 2020 by Lauren Block, MD MPH and Adam E. Block, PhD

Illustrated by Alex Brissenden
www.illus-bee.com

Blockstar Publications
www.kellystayshome.com
Kelly Goes Back to School. Downloadable via Kindle, iBooks and NOOK.

ISBN: 978-1-7349493-6-0 (soft cover)
ISBN: 978-1-7349493-7-7 (ebook)
ISBN: 978-1-7349493-8-4

Lauren D. Block MD MPH and Adam E. Block PhD
Illustrations by Alex Brissenden
Email: coronaviruschildrensbook@gmail.com
1. Juvenile fiction
2. Health & Daily Living——Diseases, Illnesses and Injuries ——United States of America with int. Distribution.

Kelly is not so excited it's Sunday night. "I am not sure I want to go back to school tomorrow, Mom," says Kelly, packing her backpack.

"Kelly," her mom says, "you love school. You have since nursery school. You'll see Eva, paint in art, and this year you will have Ms. Singh, who I hear is super nice. Home school was a unique experience, and important since coronavirus made it unsafe to all be in school together. Since there are fewer cases in our area than last spring, school will open part time this fall."

Kelly starts to smile. "I am excited to see my friends again. And to help Joey start Kindergarten."
"Yay, Kindergarten!" shouts Joey. "When you go back to school tomorrow," says Mom, "it will be a little different than school last year."

"Because I will be in Kindergarten!" says Joey. "Right," Mom says. "There are also changes you will see in school because of coronavirus. You will have fewer kids in each classroom, and tape on the floor to help you stay 6 feet apart."

"How will there be fewer kids in each class?" asks Kelly.

"This fall there will be a Monday/Tuesday session and a Thursday/Friday session at school. Half the kids will go earlier in the week, and half later in the week. Wednesday will be a cleaning day. The teachers will give you work to do those days you are not in school. This will make it safer for everyone at school."

"Will we get to play on the playground at school?" asks Joey.

"The playgrounds are open again," says Mom, "but there will not be regular recess at school, since that involves lots of kids playing close together. You'll be able to play with some kids in your class. In the afternoons and on the weekend, we can go to the playground, ride bikes, and play soccer as a family."

"What else will be different at school?" asks Kelly.
"Well," says Dad, "specials like music and art will
be in your regular classroom. You will eat lunch
in your classroom or outside, not in the cafeteria."
"Why?" asks Kelly.
"This is called *cohorting*," says Dad. "The school is
keeping a small group of kids together. Lunch or
recess with your whole grade would mean lots of
kids near each other."
"And that could spread coronavirus!" says Kelly.
"Right," says Dad.

"Just like at home, you will wash your hands, and there will be hand sanitizer to use. We will pack your backpacks with your own crayons, pencils, and markers so you will not need to share with the other kids in your class. For now, anything we touch a lot should not be shared between kids at school. When you do touch things everyone shares at school, like the pencil sharpener, it is a good idea to wash your hands after."

"Will we need to wear masks at school?" asks Joey.
"It's so hot in my mask!"
"Yes, Joey, masks are the only reason we can go to school at all! Anytime you are inside with other people not in our family, we need to wear masks, just like when we go to the supermarket or bring Spot to the vet. You can choose any superhero mask you want for the first day of school."

The past several months have taught us that masks work. Masks keep your germs in and everyone else's germs out. In studies with over twenty five thousand people, face masks and social distancing led to lower risk of *viral transmission*, or spread of the virus.

If only the teacher wears a mask, other kids who feel fine can accidentally cough or sneeze on you and get you sick. If everyone is wearing a mask, the chance of getting an infection or giving an infection to other people is much lower.

"We are also not going to share food or drinks, so we'll pack your lunch every morning. However, there is good evidence that coronavirus mostly spreads between people in the air, not on fomites."

"Fomites?" asks Kelly.

"*Fomites* mean surfaces or objects. We can all walk on the same floor, sit on the same chair or play on the same swings and you are very unlikely to catch coronavirus, especially if you keep washing your hands."

"Your temperature will be checked every morning to make sure you don't have a fever. If you do, you and Joey will stay home until you feel better."

"Wait," Kelly says, "Why does Joey have to stay home if I'm sick?" asks Kelly.

"That's a good question. We have to make sure that neither of you is going to school sick. Because it is so contagious, if one of you has it, the other might also. Most spreading happens within families."

| 0 - 9,999 | 10,000 - 49,999 | 50,000 - 99,999 | 100,000+ |

"Is it risky to go back?" asks Kelly as she brushes her teeth. "I thought that's what I heard on TV."

"Kelly, there's risk in everything we do, from riding our bikes to driving our car. Experts in *public health*, or the health of people in our community, watch the number of people getting sick every day. The government and your school feel it is safe enough to have kids, teachers, and everyone else at your school go back as long as we follow the rules."

"Not Maggie's family!" exclaims Kelly. "She got to go to camp this summer, and her family took a plane to go on vacation."

"Kelly, every family is different. Some families are more comfortable doing more things, some families have to do more things, and other families feel much less comfortable going out. Eva's family hasn't gone to a store or seen anyone since the pandemic started. Each family gets to decide. It's important that we support all our friends and family."

"So what will you, Dad, and Spot do at home when we're at school?" asks Kelly.
"Dad is going to start going into the office one day a week. He will work from home the other days. He will drive instead of taking the train to avoid being around too many people. Since everyone will be going to the office just one day a week, there will be fewer people at his office, but he will get to see some of his coworkers again."

"The days Dad goes to the office, I will be working from home doing *telehealth*. This means I will be seeing patients from home."

"Like when I saw the doctor on the computer this summer?" asks Joey.

"Exactly like that," says Mom. "I see patients by video chat. They tell me what's wrong, and sometimes I can do a physical exam to look at their eyes, mouth, or even their feet. This works well for people who are at higher risk, and for people can't go to the doctor's office."

"Since school is opening, does this mean we'll get to see Grandma and Papa again?" asks Joey, who just put on his pajamas.
"Yes," replies Mom, "Grandma and Papa are ready to see us in the backyard. We are going to have them come over this weekend to do an art project and play baseball with you. They will want to hear all about school, but we will not hug and kiss them nor share food with them."

"What about Joey's birthday next month?" asks Kelly. "We will of course have a fun fifth birthday for Joey. We can have one or two of his best friends over in the yard. We'll have games outside, play soccer, and sing to him. Now that things are opening, there are more things we can do, like see a few friends outside. We can go to stores to buy school supplies, as long as we wear a mask and wash our hands after."

"Like every year, we'll bring him for his check-up the week after his birthday at the pediatrician's office. The office is open, so we can start to go for check-ups when you need or if you get sick," Mom says. "And we get to go back to the dentist!" says Dad with a smile.

Mom sits in Kelly's bed to read her a story. Kelly feels something prickly on her arm. It is a bandage. "Mom, did you get hurt?" asks Kelly.

"No, I had to get a blood test," answers her Mom. "The test was to see if I had antibody response to COVID-19, or a response from the infection fighters in my immune system. It's called an *antibody test*."

Kelly looks confused. "Mom, I thought you said antibodies were made when you get sick or get a vaccine?"

"Good memory, Kelly!" says Mom. "Vaccines and infection are two ways your body makes an antibody response."

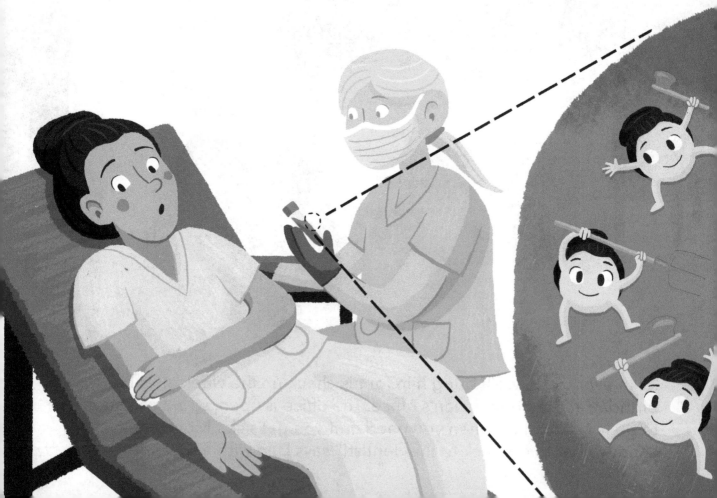

"Sometimes, though, people are lucky enough to be *asymptomatic*, or have an immune response without getting sick and without a vaccine. Since I work in healthcare taking care of people who have gotten sick with COVID-19, there's a chance I had an antibody response without knowing it. That might offer some protection against getting sick. I will still need to wear a mask and take all the precautions in the hospital though."

"Will we have to take a test?" asks Kelly. "Not right now," says her mom. "If any of the kids in your class get sick, they will have a test for coronavirus with a nose or mouth swab. If they test positive, anyone who was near them will have to stay home for about two weeks to make sure they don't get sick and transmit the infection to others."

"So the whole class will have to stay home?" asks Kelly, eyes wide.

"Yes," says their mom, "as well as their family and anyone they've been in close contact with, or around for at least 15 minutes. This is called *contact tracing*, and is a good way to make sure the infection never spreads as quickly as it did last spring. Since we are all now experts in home school, we will be able to change back and forth between regular and home school quickly should that happen."

"To make sure we are prepared in case we need to go back to home school, your teacher and I will remind you to bring anything you really need home every day. The school will let us know if certain kids need to stay home, or if the whole school needs to close again to keep the number of infections down."

Entrance

"Mom, this is a lot different than school last year!" exclaims Kelly.

"It is a big change," says Mom, "but it's important. There have been more than 14 million people sick with COVID-19 across the world as of mid-summer, 2020. Since there are fewer sick people in our area, it is tempting to think that things are back to normal and stop being as careful. But there is always the risk of a *resurgence*, or second round of infections, so we need to continue to socially distance, wear masks, and stay home if we're sick."

"When will we go back to normal school, like we had before
coronavirus?" asks Kelly.
"It will probably be a long time, possibly more than a year, before
we can go back to big parties, concerts, or shows. Looking around
the United States and the world, certain areas have very low
infection rates. Other areas in the United States, Latin America, India,
and Africa have rising rates. This is a global pandemic, which means
we are all in this together to reduce the risk of infection."

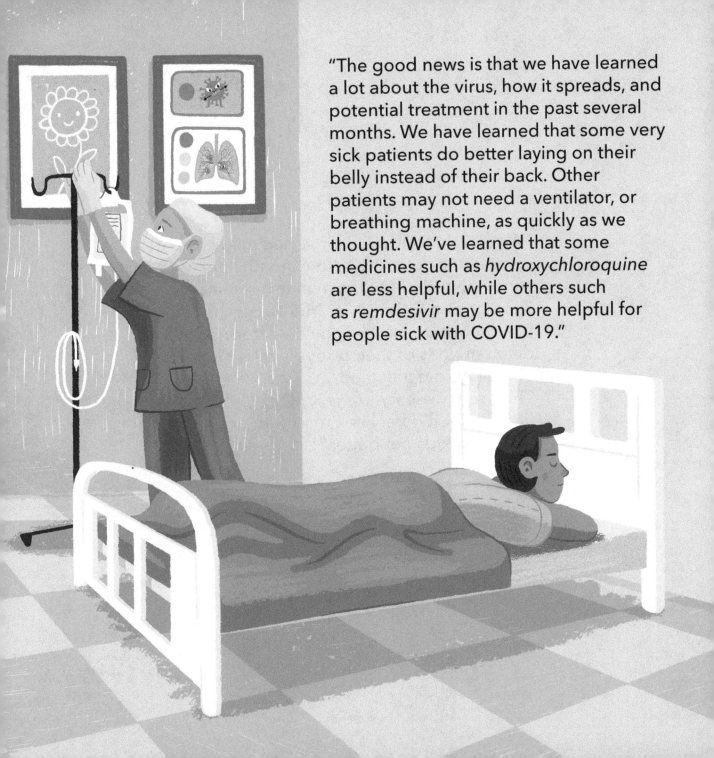

"The good news is that we have learned a lot about the virus, how it spreads, and potential treatment in the past several months. We have learned that some very sick patients do better laying on their belly instead of their back. Other patients may not need a ventilator, or breathing machine, as quickly as we thought. We've learned that some medicines such as *hydroxychloroquine* are less helpful, while others such as *remdesivir* may be more helpful for people sick with COVID-19."

"We saw that a few kids who had mild cases of coronavirus got sick about a month after, with a condition called **M**ultisystem **I**nflammatory **S**yndrome in **C**hildren, or **MIS-C**. For these kids, several weeks after they recover from COVID-19, different parts of their body, like their heart, skin, or kidneys get inflamed."

"That sounds scary!" says Kelly.

"Thankfully it is very rare, and with good medical care most kids get better."

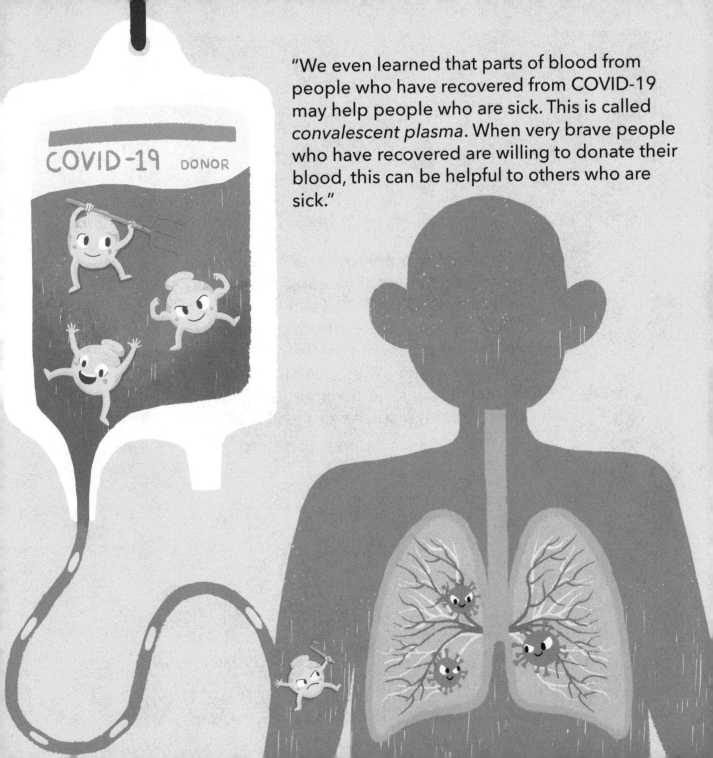

"We even learned that parts of blood from people who have recovered from COVID-19 may help people who are sick. This is called *convalescent plasma*. When very brave people who have recovered are willing to donate their blood, this can be helpful to others who are sick."

"Through the antibody testing, like I just got, we will see how many people have some immunity to COVID-19. In some areas less than 5% of people have antibodies, and in other areas, about 20% of people have antibodies. Once we get to a high percentage of people with antibodies, *herd immunity* will help prevent further spread of the illness."

"Meanwhile, scientists are doing *trials*, or tests, of new vaccines against COVID-19. These are looking promising, but have to be tested in lots of people to make sure they are safe and effective, which means they will not hurt you and they work well to prevent the illness. Once we know these vaccines work well, the government will need to get these to everyone, which takes a long time."

"Until then, we will keep having fun together and making the best of the small things, like going back to school and Dad going back to the office." Their dog barks. "I think Spot is going to be happy to have us gone every day," says Kelly. She grabs her backpack and puts it by the door. "I think I'm ready for 4th grade," says Kelly.

"I *know* you are," says her mom, smiling.